SUPER BOWL CHAMPIONS
ST. LOUIS RAMS

LINEBACKER
JAMES LAURINAITIS

SUPER BOWL CHAMPIONS

ST. LOUIS RAMS

AARON FRISCH

CREATIVE EDUCATION

Published by Creative Education
P.O. Box 227, Mankato, Minnesota 56002
Creative Education is an imprint of The Creative Company
www.thecreativecompany.us

Design and production by Blue Design
Art direction by Rita Marshall
Printed in the United States of America

Photographs by Corbis (Walter Bibikow/JAI), Getty
Images (Brian Bahr, Andrew D. Bernstein, Kevin C. Cox,
Whitney Curtis, Jay Drowns, Paul Jasienski, Lonnie Major/
Allsport, Al Messerschmidt/NFL, Ronald C. Modra/Sports
Imagery, NFL Photos, Vic Stein/NFL, Kevin Terrell)

Library of Congress Cataloging-in-Publication Data
Frisch, Aaron.
St. Louis Rams / Aaron Frisch.
p. cm. — (Super bowl champions)
Includes index.
Summary: An elementary look at the St. Louis Rams
professional football team, including its formation in
Cleveland in 1937, most memorable players, Super Bowl
championship, and stars of today.
ISBN 978-1-60818-386-9
1. St. Louis Rams (Football team)—History—Juvenile
literature. I. Title.

GV956.S85F76 2014
796.332'640977866—dc23   2013014837

First Edition
9 8 7 6 5 4 3 2 1

2012 RAMS DEFENSE

FAMOUS RAMS

MERLIN OLSEN / 1962-76

Merlin was a defensive tackle. He was part of a defensive line called the "Fearsome Foursome."

TABLE OF CONTENTS

JACK YOUNGBLOOD / 1971–84

Jack was a defensive end who always played his hardest. He made the Pro Bowl seven times.

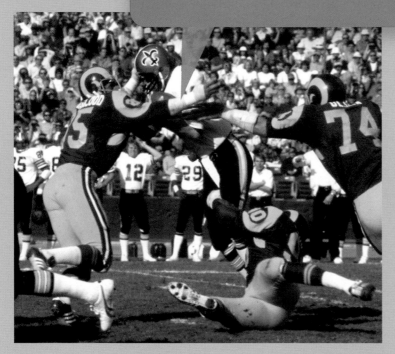

THE FIGHTING RAMS

In 1937, Cleveland, Ohio, got a football team called the Rams. Rams are male sheep with big, curly horns. The Rams have been fighting on the football field ever since!

8

ERIC DICKERSON / 1983–87

Eric was a fast running back. In 1983, he carried the ball for 2,105 yards as just a **rookie**!

WELCOME TO ST. LOUIS

St. Louis is a city in Missouri. In the 1800s, many **settlers** went through St. Louis as they traveled to the West. St. Louis has a huge monument called the Gateway Arch.

QUARTERBACK
BOB WATERFIELD

A LOT OF MOVES

The Rams have played in three different cities in
their history. They started in Cleveland. Then they
moved to Los Angeles, California. In 1995, the Rams
moved to St. Louis.

HALFBACK
KENNY WASHINGTON

13

ELROY HIRSCH

THE RAMS' STORY

The Rams were born in Cleveland. Quarterback Bob Waterfield helped them win the National Football League (NFL) championship in 1945. Then the Rams moved to Los Angeles.

Wide receiver Elroy Hirsch was a star for Los Angeles. He ran so fast that fans called him "Crazylegs." Elroy helped the Rams win the 1951 championship.

1948 RAMS

15

MARSHALL FAULK / 1999-2006

Marshall was a quick and **shifty** running back. He helped St. Louis win Super Bowl XXXIV.

SOUND IT OUT

FAULK: *FAHK*

In the 1960s, the Rams had tough defensive linemen. Los Angeles got to the **playoffs** many times in the 1970s and 1980s. But it could not win the Super Bowl.

16

KEVIN GREENE / 1985–92

Kevin was a fierce linebacker. After he quit playing football, he did some professional wrestling!

"If you put the
ball in position
to catch it, they
catch it."
—KURT WARNER

TORRY HOLT

he Rams got better after they moved to St. Louis. Quarterback Kurt Warner led them to Super Bowl XXXIV (34). They beat the Tennessee Titans to become world champs!

St. Louis had a lot of fast players like wide receiver Torry Holt in the early 2000s. Fans said the Rams were "The Greatest Show on Turf"!

CHRIS LONG / 2008–present

Chris was a defensive end. He was big but very fast. His dad Howie had been an NFL star, too.

y 2013, quarterback Sam Bradford was leading the Rams' offense. Fans hoped that Sam and the Rams would soon fight their way to another Super Bowl!

FACTS FILE

CONFERENCE/DIVISION:
National Football
Conference, West Division

TEAM COLORS:
Gold and blue

HOME STADIUM:
Edward Jones Dome

SUPER BOWL VICTORY:
XXXIV, January 30, 2000
  23–16 over Tennessee
  Titans

NFL WEBSITE FOR KIDS:
http://nflrush.com

RUNNING BACK
STEVEN JACKSON

GLOSSARY

playoffs — games that the best teams play after a season to see who the champion will be

Pro Bowl — a special game after the season that only the best NFL players get to play

rookie — a player in his first season

settlers — people who move into wild areas to build homes there

shifty — able to change directions quickly while moving

INDEX